PARABLES OF JESUS

THE RECKLESS SON

Retold by Susan Dickinson
Illustrated by Amanda Hall

CARNIVAL

Many people thought that Jesus should only have friends who were good people. They didn't approve when he talked to people they considered idle cheats. So Jesus told them a story.

Once upon a time there was a man who had two sons. One day the younger son said, "Father, I know that when you die your farm will be divided between my brother and me. But I want my share now." So the man divided his farm in two and gave half to his younger son.

But in a very short time the young man decided to sell his share of the farm and make a lot of money. He wanted to travel abroad, instead of working hard in the fields all day.

It was wonderful having plenty of money to spend. He dined in expensive eating places and entertained friends wherever he went.

But of course, eventually he spent all his money. He soon discovered that his new friends weren't really friends at all. As soon as they saw he could no longer afford to pay, they disappeared.

Now that all his money had gone, the young man had to find work. But this was not easy and the only job he could get was with a farmer who needed somebody to look after his pigs.

He was hardly paid anything and he had to live in a little low hut near the animals. Soon he was so hungry he felt like eating the bean pods that were given to the pigs.

While he sat watching the pigs rooting about under the trees, he began to think. "What a fool I've been. I've spent all my money. I'm half starving. My own father's servants are better off than I am. I'll give up this job, go home to my father and say how sorry I am that I've behaved so badly. Perhaps he'll let me work on his farm as a servant."

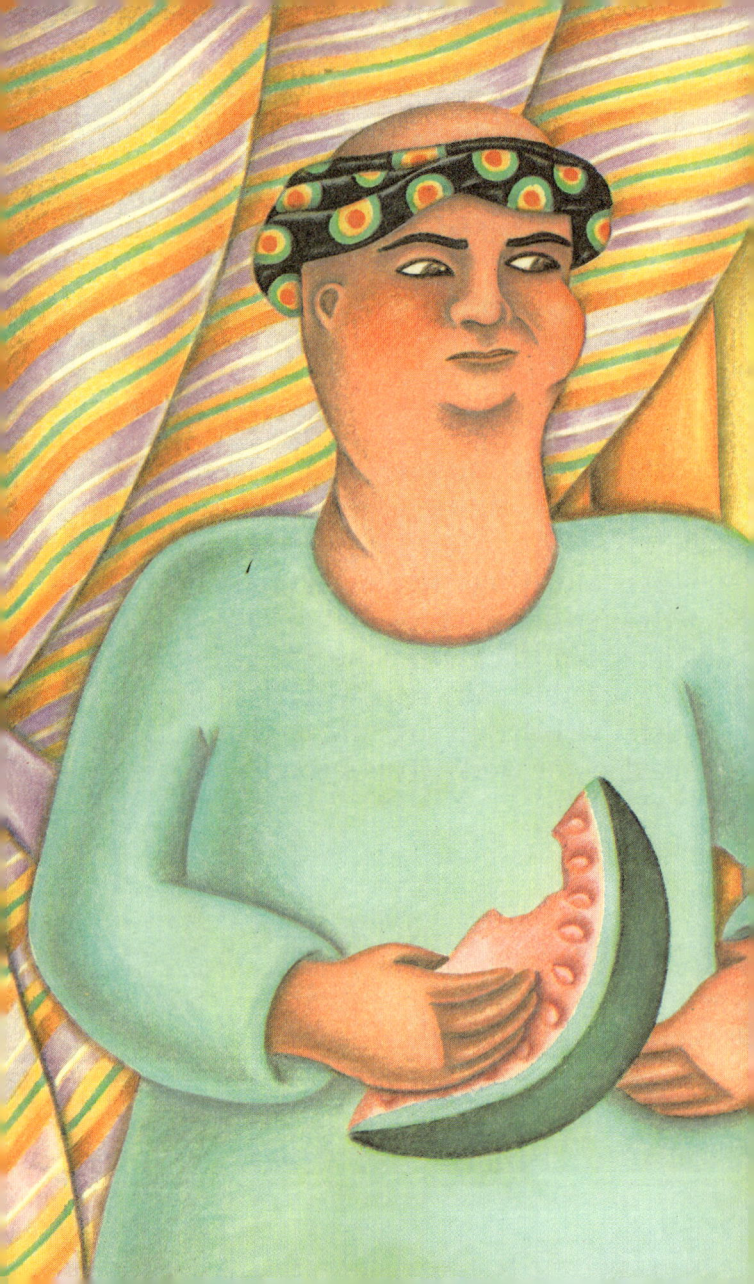

So the young man told his master he was going home to his father and he started out on the long journey to his father's farm.

At last, footsore and weary, he came within sight of his home. His father spied him coming from far off and ran to meet him.

The father threw his arms around his son and hugged him warmly. But the young man hung his head. "I'm sorry, Father," he said. "I've been a fool. I'm not fit to be called your son."

"Nonsense!" cried his father. "Bring my son some fresh clothes and new shoes," he called to his servants. "Bring a ring for his finger. Then go and kill the best calf and prepare a feast. For this son of mine was nearly dead, but now he's alive. He was lost and has now been found."

In the meantime, the elder brother was still hard at work in the fields. When he came home in the evening, he heard music and singing. He called out to one of the servants, "What's going on?"

"Your brother has come home," the servant replied. "And your father told us to prepare a great feast because he has come back to us."

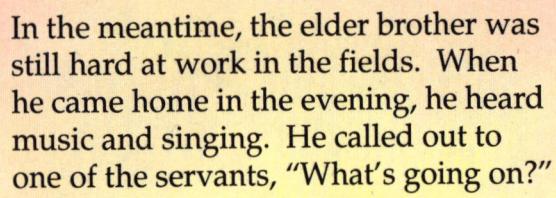

The elder brother was so angry he refused to go indoors. Eventually his father came out to look for him and begged him to come in.

"I've worked hard in the fields for years. I've done what you told me to do and never complained," the elder brother burst out. "And you haven't even given me a goat for a barbecue with my friends. My brother wasted all the money he made after selling his share of the farm. He just went off and enjoyed himself. Now that he's decided to come home at last, you throw a party! It isn't fair!"

The father put his hands on his elder son's shoulders. "My boy," he said. "You have always been here with me and everything I have is yours. You know that. But we have to celebrate and be happy because your brother was as good as dead and is now alive. He was lost and now has been found."